The Fountain of Life

Contemplating God

Edited by Matthew Barrett

The Fountain of Life: Contemplating the Aseity of God, Samuel G. Parkison

The Fountain of Life

Contemplating the Aseity of God

Samuel G. Parkison

WHEATON, ILLINOIS

The Fountain of Life: Contemplating the Aseity of God

Published by Crossway
1300 Crescent Street
Wheaton, Illinois 60187

Cover design: David Fassett

Cover images: Getty Images, Rawpixel, and Wikimedia Commons

First printing 2026

Printed in the United States of America

All emphases in Scripture quotations have been added by the author.

Trade paperback ISBN: 978-8-8749-0082-3
ePub ISBN: 978-8-8749-0084-7
PDF ISBN: 978-8-8749-0083-0

Library of Congress Cataloging-in-Publication Data

Names: Parkison, Samuel G. author
Title: The fountain of life : contemplating the aseity of God / Samuel G. Parkison.
Description: Wheaton, Illinois : Crossway, 2026. | Series: Contemplating God | Includes bibliographical references and index.
Identifiers: LCCN 2025004021 (print) | LCCN 2025004022 (ebook) | ISBN 9798874900823 (trade paperback) | ISBN 9798874900830 (pdf) | ISBN 9798874900847 (epub)
Subjects: LCSH: God (Christianity)—Eternity | God (Christianity)—Immutability
Classification: LCC BT153.I47 P37 2026 (print) | LCC BT153.I47 (ebook)
LC record available at https://lccn.loc.gov/2025004021
LC ebook record available at https://lccn.loc.gov/2025004022

Crossway is a publishing ministry of Good News Publishers.

VP 35 34 33 32 31 30 29 28 27 26
15 14 13 12 11 10 9 8 7 6 5 4 3 2 1

Contents

Series Preface

About Credo

Credo exists to retrieve classical Christianity for the sake of creating and cultivating reformation in the church today. *Credo* is Latin for "I believe." In our age of unbelief, Credo says, "I believe." From the creeds of the church fathers to the confessions of the Reformers, Christians have faithfully confessed the faith across the church catholic (universal). By bridging the gap between church and academy, Credo helps churchgoers, pastors, and students alike retrieve classical Christianity for the sake of biblical and orthodox fidelity, fostering theological renewal in the church today. Credo invites you to read *Credo Magazine*, listen to the Credo podcast, and participate in the Credo Conference. To that end, as the founder of Credo, I now invite you to pick up and read Credo's Contemplating God series published by Crossway.

About the Series

Christians are called to confess the faith "once for all delivered to the saints" (Jude 3). This does not mean merely adhering to dusty, old articulations of the faith in a lifeless or dull manner. The best articulations of Christianity that have been passed down through the ages are not dull; they are unimaginably vibrant because the God whom they describe is the plentitude of life. In our call to confess the faith once for all delivered to the saints, we are invited to "gaze upon the beauty of the Lord" (Ps. 27:4) and to sit at the feet of the Lord Jesus, learning from him and enjoying his presence (Luke 10:39).

This kind of meditation on the glory of God is what Christians throughout the centuries have called "contemplation." It is marked by humility as we stand *coram Deo*, before the incomprehensible splendor and infinite blessedness of our God. Unfortunately, books written for the express purpose of contemplating God and his glory are far too rare. Contemplation was the hallmark of classical Christian theology, but now we moderns imagine theology is worthwhile only to the degree of its "utility" in "practical" daily living. Theology, for many of us, has become a means to some other lesser end.

The books in Credo's Contemplating God series strive to cast a different vision for theology and the Christian life. They invite readers to wonder at the majesty of our triune God not as some means to another end but as *the greatest end itself*. After all, to "glorify God and enjoy him forever" is *the* chief end of man (Westminster Shorter Catechism, question 1). To joyfully gaze upon the beauty of God is our ultimate purpose, as creatures made in his image. Whatever else we look forward to in the eternal rest of the new heavens and the new earth, this enjoyment of God will be central to our everlasting experience.

Thus, these brief meditations do not concern matters peripheral to the Christian life. They are kindling for the fire of worship, which is at the *heart* of the Christian life. Without sacrificing depth, the authors of this series condense their wisdom for the everyday Christian who may not have previous familiarity with technical theological language. In the spirit of C. S. Lewis, that great popularizer of profound truths, these essays seek to be both informative and enjoyable. Every book in the Contemplating God series is a reflection on God that invites the reader to gaze on the beauty of our Lord. Each book is also an invitation to listen to the profundity of the Great Tradition—apostolic teaching handed down by the historic church through her confession and worship of the triune God. The chronological snobbery Lewis so detested is not welcomed here. We are not the first to climb this mountain, nor do we dare to do so alone. For the faith we confess is one that has been delivered *to the saints*. In that spirit, I pray God will use these books to bless the church with an eyeful of his glory.

Matthew Barrett
TRINITY ANGLICAN SEMINARY

1

More Eternal

CHILDREN OFTEN ASK the best philosophical questions. The reason is hinted at by the etymology of the word *philosophy*. Philosophy is the love of wisdom. And children—unaccustomed to the tyranny of the urgent that often comes with adulthood and its wonder-thieving stodginess—are usually aware of no other reason to ask a question than to sincerely *know the answer*. It does not occur to them to ask useful questions, or practical questions, or intelligent questions. Rather, they ask the questions—and *only* the questions—to which they want answers.

Among the many virtues our Lord was commending when he urged us to become like little children (Matt. 18:3), surely this must have been one of them: a genuine delight in asking questions to be answered. Another insight we learn from children's questions is that the best philosophical questions are also irreducibly theological in nature. For good reason, Solomon—that great philosopher-theologian-poet-king—declared that "the fear of the LORD is the beginning of wisdom" (Prov. 9:10). Children know this. As soon as they become conscious of God, they intuitively direct all manner of questions to *him*, including those questions that grown-ups are too embarrassed to ask—like Why did God make us need to go to the bathroom? Or Why did God make sugar bad for us if it tastes so good? Or Why did God make boogers?

I was reminded of this childlike virtue—of asking a question for no other reason than the desire to have it answered—when my eight-year-old son offered a question of the highest philosophical and theological caliber. The two of us were on a couch, slouched and unhurried. We were talking about nothing memorable or noteworthy. Whatever preceded his question in our conversation is dialogue that has been lost to the annals of history—another example of the seemingly infinite, forgettable plot points God delights to providentially write into his story of human history. Without any indication that he was changing the conversation from the mundane to the profound, he asked, "Dad, if God is eternal, and if being eternal for him means that he had no beginning or end, and if Jesus gives *us* eternal life, but we *do* have a beginning, does that mean that he is *more* eternal than us?" This, dear reader, is philosophy at its best. This is theology at its most mysterious. Don't let the simplicity of his question fool you into missing its profundity. Maybe we can see how deeply profound it is by putting it into the form of a syllogism:

> Premise 1: God is eternal.
> Premise 2: God's eternity means that he has no beginning or end.
> Premise 3: Jesus grants us eternal life.
> Premise 4: Even though our life (like God's) has no end, it had a beginning (unlike God's).
> Possible conclusion: God is *more* eternal than the eternal life he gives us.

Now, of course, my son did not need to formalize his line of inquiry in such a way because his question was not an artificial thought experiment. It was relevant for him right there on the surface of his daily thought life. His was a question tapping into the nature of reality itself. I suspect that this is why it did not feel jarring for him to shift suddenly from whatever we were talking about to a question of God's eternality in relation to the eternal life he grants us in Christ. My son has a better sense of what's going on than most of us in the sense that he intuitively knows what we grown-ups need to remind ourselves of: None of our questions, conversations, or experiences are *ever* really disconnected from the reality of God and his eternity. In truth, my son took no sharp turn when he shifted from talking about his favorite food (or what he was looking forward to doing that afternoon, or what he had learned in school earlier, or whatever we were talking about) to asking about eternal life in Christ and God's eternity. He went from talking about reality to talking about *ultimate* reality, which only feels like a sharp turn for those of us who have forgotten that all the best questions—that is, the ones we ask because we want to know the answers—all have very natural pathways to questions about God, for "in him we live and move and have our being" (Acts 17:28).

Well, I didn't have a chance to answer this question before my son complexified it further with an additional, contingent question: "And if God is *more* eternal than us," he continued to think aloud, "what does it even mean that our life is eternal?" In other words, my son had intuited that the possible answer to his question—his provisional thesis that God is *more* eternal than us—was in danger of equivocation. What does "eternal" even mean if you can have *more* or *less* of it? What good is it to use the same word to describe both us and God if "eternity" means one thing for us and something altogether different for him? Are we forced to secretly toggle between definitions of the word "eternal" just to avoid a direct self-contradiction? These are deep realities here!

Now, the only thing that matches the intoxicating wonder of a child's philosophical or theological question is the correct answer. In this case, I'm uncertain whether my answer landed in my son's mind with as much force as his question landed in mine, but if it didn't, it wasn't due to any lack of wonderful intrigue in the answer itself (but probably due to my inability to appropriately highlight its profundity). In truth, yes, we do mean different things when we describe God's eternal life and our eternal life. They are connected by way of analogy. We can come to share in the eternal life of God by gift—but we are still creatures experiencing something creaturely. Our eternal life in the life of God is *derived*—but his is not so. He *is* eternal life. The worshipful truth that answers my son's excellent question is that God the Trinity—the eternal fire of vitality, love, and radiance that ever burns as Father, Son, and Spirit—*is* eternal life. God is life *in himself.* And what he is by nature, he grants for us to share by grace. We will never be those who have eternal life in and of ourselves—our eternal life is always a begraced share in a vitality that never began and will never end.

This truth of God's eternal life has a theological name: *aseity*, which simply means that God's life is from himself (the word derives from Latin—the prefix *a* means "from," and *se* means "self"). But of course, when I say, "which simply means," I am not at all attempting to demystify the mystery. When we are dazzled by a doctrine, we must be sure to avoid robbing its luster or dimming its brilliance or dulling its penetrating sharpness by slapping a cheap technical term on it. That's not what theological terms are for. Rather, they are stand-ins for the mysteries of God. Far be it from me to explain away the depths of God in shallow fashion. Should we find ourselves awestruck, for example, by the eternal life that *is* God's vital existence, the word *aseity* should not function to conveniently diminish that awe—as if to say, "Ah, I see. I thought this was deeply mysterious, but it turns out that there's a word for this thing: *aseity*. Now the mystery is solved." Rather, theological language preserves mystery for the sake of worship. Instead of diminishing feelings of humble awe, wonder, and worship, the word *aseity* should conjure up all these feelings! The word should make your skin tingle and stop your breath.

Over the course of this book, we shall give ourselves to contemplating God's aseity, and our goal is to be moved by wonder at its mention. As we consider this divine attribute, I invite you to adopt the attitude of a child, asking a question for the sheer joy of getting its answer. You will find, I trust, that this doctrine will certainly encourage you in your Christian walk. It will, in other words, bear practical fruit in your life. But I urge you, dear reader, to resist the temptation of letting these practical effects be the motivation for learning about divine aseity. Resist the temptation to put a utilitarian requirement on this doctrine—as if the time spent meditating on it is only worth the use it will be for your practical life.

Let the meditation on this divine attribute be an end in itself. Let us become familiar with the sentiments of Jonathan Edwards when he read 1 Timothy 1:17 as a young man: "To the King of the ages, immortal, invisible, the only God, be honor and glory forever and ever. Amen." Recounting the experience of being moved by this passage, Edwards writes,

> As I read the words, there came into my soul, and was as it were diffused through it, a sense of the glory of the Divine Being; a new sense, quite different from any thing I ever experienced before. Never any words of scripture seemed to me as these words did. I thought with myself, how excellent a Being that was, and how happy I should be, if I might enjoy that God, and be rapt up to him in heaven, and be as it were swallowed up in him.[1]

In truth, there is nothing more practical than contemplating God, since this is the very thing we were created for as human beings. "Man's *chief* end [or purpose]," says the Westminster Shorter Catechism, "is to glorify God, and to enjoy him forever."[2] If this is true, then taking time to be dumbstruck by the majesty and wonder of God's aseity is not a distraction from practical living but, rather, material to the very purpose God made you for! To contemplate God is not a break from the real world; it is an exercise in reality.

1 Jonathan Edwards, "Personal Narrative," in *Letters and Personal Writings*, ed. George S. Claghorn, vol. 16 of *The Works of Jonathan Edwards* (Yale University Press, 1998), 792.

2 "The Westminster Shorter Catechism," in *Creeds, Confessions, and Catechisms: A Reader's Edition*, ed. Chad Van Dixhoorn (Crossway, 2022), 411.

2

Creation's Independent Creator

AT WHAT POINT does Holy Scripture introduce us to this attribute called *aseity*? In a sense, it never does; it doesn't introduce divine aseity because it's always assuming it. This attribute of God is the imposing context of all his works and self-revelation. Aseity calls attention to itself in the first words of Scripture: "In the beginning, *God created* the heavens and the earth" (Gen. 1:1). God created all that was not God "out of nothing"—*ex nihilo* in Latin. To be a creation is to be created by a Creator. Another way of saying this is that to be created is to be dependent on God for existence. This may sound unnecessarily obvious, but sometimes we forget to be properly wowed by the obvious. If creation's trademark is to be utterly dependent on its Creator for its existence, what does that imply for God and his existence? It implies that he, as the one who caused creation's existence, is essentially and existentially independent of his creation. We need him, but he does not need us at all.

The independence of God is assumed throughout the Scriptures when he contrasts himself to his creatures and their idols. Consider the example of Job, who famously questioned God and received a direct answer to his challenge. From within the whirlwind of God's answer—with Job cowering appropriately under the awesome weight of the sovereign Lord speaking to him—God asks him,

> Who has first given to me, that I should repay him?
> Whatever is under the whole heaven is mine.
> (Job 41:11)

In other words, "I'm not like you. I can't be enriched or diminished. I can't be owed or indebted—everything is mine and testifies to its being mine."

Of course, Job, if he had paid better attention, might have known this already. God's glory—his altogether unmatched and incomparable status as the independent Creator—is declared not only in the whirlwind but also through day and night:

> The heavens declare the glory of God,
> and the sky above proclaims his handiwork.
> Day to day pours out speech,
> and night to night reveals knowledge.

There is no speech, nor are there words,
whose voice is not heard.
Their voice goes out through all the earth,
and their words to the end of the world.
In them he has set a tent for the sun,
which comes out like a bridegroom leaving his chamber,
and, like a strong man, runs its course with joy.
Its rising is from the end of the heavens,
and its circuit to the end of them,
and there is nothing hidden from its heat.
(Ps. 19:1–6)

Commenting on these verses, the fourth-century church father Gregory of Nyssa writes,

> The heavens, showing the Maker's wisdom, practically shout with a voice, though silent, they declare the Creator's craftsmanship. We can hear the heavens teach us: "O mortals, in looking on us and seeing our beauty and vastness, our incessant orbit with its orderly, harmonious movement, acting in one methodical direction, turn your thoughts to our Ruler! Through the beauty you see, envisage the beauty of the unseen Source!"[1]

1 Gregory of Nyssa, "Answers to Enomius' Second Book," in *Dogmatic Treatises*, in vol. 5 of *Nicene and Post-Nicene Fathers of the Christian Church*, Series 2, ed. Philip Schaff and Henry Wace (Eerdmans, 1954), 272–73.

Where there is day, where there is night, where there are heavens and the sky above, this message can be "heard." Throughout the earth, God makes himself known through his handiwork. And what his dependent creation demonstrates is that he himself is independent. Creation needs him, but he needs not creation. Or again, consider the words of David in Psalm 24:1–2:

> The earth is the LORD's and the fullness thereof,
>   the world and those who dwell therein,
> for he has founded it upon the seas
>   and established it upon the rivers.

What do we learn from these few words? We learn that the cosmos has a Master. The earth does not simply happen to exist, and we do not simply happen to find ourselves here. Nothing that exists at all exists independently of the sovereign creative craftmanship and sustaining grace of God. God alone exists independently of anyone and anything. His existence is essential; ours is contingent and derivative. We are conditioned by him, but he is not conditioned by us. This means that whatever disparity lies between anything in the whole realm of creation and us, it does not even remotely approximate the distance between God and everything else—he alone is *owner* in an ultimate sense. This is why the Puritan pastor John Owen says,

> What is an angel more than a worm? A worm is a creature, and an angel is no more; he hath made the one to creep in

> the earth—made also the other to dwell in heaven. There is still a proportion between these, they agree in something; but what are all the nothings of the world to the God infinitely blessed for evermore?[2]

In other words, as lofty a creature as an angel is, it is still infinitely closer to a worm than to God because it is a creature. Compared to God, worms and angels are "nothings." They are part of the "fullness" of the earth that belongs to God (Ps. 24:10). Think about this word "fullness." It is an exhaustive word. Every bit of wisdom ever discovered in human history is the Lord's. Every bit of wealth ever accrued is the Lord's. Every bit of joy ever experienced is the Lord's. Every bit of food consumed, music heard, or equation solved exists within the parameters of this "fullness" that does not belong to itself—it is the Lord's. Does this not whet the appetite for discovery? Are you not thirsty to seek and find the treasures of the earth that belong to the Lord? When "the earth . . . and the fullness thereof" belong not to the impersonal domain of chance but, rather, to Yahweh—the Lord—our search for truth and beauty is given a profound justification. We look out into the world with questions expecting to find answers. We look for reason and find it. We look for order and, behold, it's there!

Furthermore, this fact ought to fill us with gratitude. For if the earth is the Lord's and the fullness thereof, what do we have

2 John Owen, *The Works of John Owen* (Banner of Truth Trust, 1965), 2:60.

that we have not received? We are, purely and exhaustively, recipients. All we do is receive, receive, receive, and our great benefactor gives and gives and gives. It is all gift! Another way to say this is that creation has its being by participation in the likeness of its Creator. What God has in and of himself (life and being), creation has by gratuitous participation in God.

If we are awake to the sheer independence of God and, therefore, to the sheer generosity of creation, we will find that we become far more interested in . . . everything. We will come to embrace what G. K. Chesterton calls "the ethics of Elfland." This is the name Chesterton gave to the outlook on reality he learned from fairy stories, which, he says,

> founded in me two convictions; first, that this world is a wild and startling place, which might have been quite different, but which is quite delightful; second, that before this wildness and delight one may well be modest and submit to the queerest limitations of so queer a kindness. But I found the whole modern world running like a high tide against both my tendernesses; and the shock of that collision created two sudden and spontaneous sentiments, which I have had ever since and which, crude as they were, have since hardened into convictions.
>
> First, I found the whole modern world talking scientific fatalism; saying that everything is as it must always have been, being unfolded without fault from the beginning. The leaf on the tree is green because it could never have

> been anything else. Now, the fairy-tale philosopher is glad that the leaf is green precisely because it might have been scarlet. He feels as if it had turned green an instant before he looked at it. He is pleased that snow is white on the strictly reasonable ground that it might have been black.[3]

What Chesterton puts his finger on is the simple fact that since the cosmos is fundamentally *contingent* and *dependent* on an independent Creator—who made the world simply and freely as a result of his own good pleasure—it is therefore fundamentally *accidental*. Now, this term "accidental" should not be contrasted with "intentional," as we typically use it today, as if God created the world by mistake. In philosophical jargon, "accidental" is contrasted with "essential." Your hair, for example, is accidental to your essence—it does not make you, *you*, and you can lose it with no consequence to the essence of *you*. Your soul, however, is essential to your essence. Humans may or may not have hair—but humans, in order to *be* humans, must have souls. However, although having a soul is essential to being human as created by God, it is not actually essential that humans exist. When we say that all of creation is, in one sense, accidental, we mean that it is not necessary. Ultimate Being does not need creation, is not enriched by creation, and would not be diminished by its cessation. This is because God *is* ultimate Being, and he is in need of nothing. Should he

3 G. K. Chesterton, *Orthodoxy* (1908; repr., Barns & Noble, 2007), 49–50.

loose the cords of dependence and let the tapestry of creation unravel into oblivion, the fullness of his own being would not be impacted at all, because his being never depended and cannot depend on that tapestry.

Since, then, creation itself is marvelously dispensable—since it does not have to exist at all, let alone exist in this way—we are invited to be amazed by all of it. We are invited to look at elephants and simply wonder at the fact that God made them look (somehow) hilariously grave and glorious. And they are all the more wonderful because they did not have to be that way (or to be at all). We are invited to positively delight in the sheer quiddity—the indelible "thisness"—of everything. The taste of coffee, the scratch of pen on paper, the smell of new books, and everything else we experience in our mundane lives are wonders precisely because they don't have to be the way they are; it is a marvel that they are this way rather than that way or not at all. We can agree with Chesterton when he says, "Now I deny most energetically that anything is, or can be, uninteresting."[4]

However, in light of the grandeur of God's independence and the fodder for worshipful wonder that creation is by consequence, the idolization of creation is all the more scandalous. In the Scriptures, God brings this application of his independence home to the attendant reader in tragically humorous

4 G. K. Chesterton, *In Defense of Sanity: The Best Essays of G. K. Chesterton*, ed. Dale Ahlquist, Joseph Peace, and Aiden Mackey (Ignatius, 2011), 36.

ways. In Isaiah 44:9–20, God speaks through his prophet Isaiah to shame his people Israel for their idolatry. The idolater—that is, the one who worships *not God* (which could be anything) as God—is involved in a self-inflicted insanity that is only made apparent by satire. God talks about the ironsmith who ironically makes himself tired in the creation of an idol he hopes will deliver him (Isa. 44:12). He also describes the carpenter who

> cuts down cedars, or he chooses a cypress tree or an oak and lets it grow strong among the trees of the forest. He plants a cedar and the rain nourishes it. Then it becomes fuel for a man. He takes a part of it and warms himself; he kindles a fire and bakes bread. Also he makes a god and worships it; he makes it an idol and falls down before it. Half of it he burns in the fire. Over the half he eats meat; he roasts it and is satisfied. Also he warms himself and says, "Aha, I am warm, I have seen the fire!" And the rest of it he makes into a god, his idol, and falls down to it and worships it. He prays to it and says, "Deliver me, for you are my god!" (Isa. 44:14–17)

"Behold the idolater," God effectively says, "see the brilliant ingenuity of a guy who makes himself a god, carries it around, and then asks for *it* to help *him*! This is truly a bold strategy, one too sophisticated for the simple worshiper to try. He has to do the incredible feat of entrusting himself to a god entirely dependent on him. How impressive! How wise!" God calls attention to the scandalous folly of trading worship of the one who carries and sustains all things for the worship of a pitiful thing that must itself be carried and sustained. Not in vain does the prophet Jeremiah call this trade appalling:

> Be appalled, O heavens, at this;
> be shocked, be utterly desolate, declares the LORD,
> for my people have committed two evils:
> they have forsaken me,
> the fountain of living waters,
> and hewed out cisterns for themselves,
> broken cisterns that can hold no water. (Jer. 2:12–13)

In all these ways, Scripture makes apparent this breathtaking reality: What distinguishes God from all else is that he alone is absolutely independent. This last Scripture quotation is illustrative: The idolatrous cisterns we carve out ourselves are unable to sustain water (with water being a sign of life—our self-made gods cannot save, sustain, or provide for us), and they are contrasted not with a divine cistern that has some water of life to draw from but, rather, with God who is the fountain of living waters. All life comes from him who is a boundless plentitude of life. There is no mutual dependence between us and God—or between God and lesser gods. All that is *not God* owes its existence *to* God. And, crucially, this order can never be reversed.

When Paul was at the Areopagus in Athens, he addressed the Stoics—the philosophical school that believed that the divine logos (or "reason") runs through all of creation (similar to what we today call *pantheism*, the belief that all of creation *is* God). Paul used a line from a Stoic poem against the Stoic conception of the divine. Rather than pamper the Stoics in their puny portrayal of God as radically connected to and contained within creation, Paul baptized a Stoic phrase to reinforce the independent transcendence of God: "In him we live and move and have our being" (Acts 17:28). We creatures owe all that we are to God. But living and moving and having our being in him does not mean that *he* lives and moves and has his being *in us*.

This relation of dependence and contingency is entirely one-sided: We need God, but he does not need us. Now, this may seem simple enough, but the implications are more radical (and frankly, more uncomfortable) than most of us tend to think. And we will have ample opportunities to highlight some of these implications in due course.

Presently, though, we ought to consider God's aseity from another angle. Until now, our reflections have been primarily negative in the sense that we are describing what God is *not* (i.e., he is not dependent). God is *a se* (that is, "from himself"—he has the attribute of aseity) because he is *independent*—he needs nothing and no one. But Scripture also affirms this doctrine of aseity positively. In other words, it is not simply that God needs nothing; it is rather the case that he needs nothing *because* he is the plentitude of life! And so a consideration of God's boundless fullness of life and being is what we must now give ourselves to.

3

I AM

PICTURE A MEDITERRANEAN SHEPHERD in the ancient Near East tending his flock of sheep as they wander a mountainous wilderness. This is a skill the shepherd likely learned from his father-in-law who owns these sheep since the shepherd is a foreigner in this land. Having arrived as a fugitive from Egypt just west of this wilderness, our shepherd had to learn many skills to adjust to his new home. Born a slave and raised by an Egyptian princess, this man has grown with a certain kind of ambition. While his upbringing was royal, he had identified with his marginalized kinsmen. Since he had come from means, he likely would have been able to gather as much information about his familial heritage as was available, but there were probably minimal written records at this point. Instead, he would have learned the oral traditions of his people.

Like everyone at that time, these people had their own account of the creation of the cosmos, the deluge of the earth, and the subsequent growth of peoples and civilizations. But unlike the creation account of their enslavers or the other great peoples of that region of the world, these people, the kinsmen of the shepherd, believed that the world did not come about as the aftermath of a cosmic war between various gods or the ordering of preexistent primordial chaos. Rather, they believed that a single God created the cosmos not by rearranging preexistent material but, rather, by speaking it into existence. Again, however, there were likely only fragments of a written account of these things at the time, and this marginalized group of slaves did not have a "canon of Scripture" to study or meditate on. They had stories. Stories about how God had called their forefather, a man named Abraham, to leave his people and their idols to venture out on his own to become the father of a great nation. Stories about how this God had entered into covenant with Abraham and his descendants. Stories about how this God appeared from time to time to interact with Abraham's posterity—a dream of a stairway to heaven, a wrestling match with the divine, familial betrayals, and divine deliverances.

All these stories may have floated around in the mind of the shepherd like so many dandelion seeds in a strong gust while he lived in Egypt. Perhaps he considered it his destiny to lead his people out of slavery when, one day as a young man, he killed an Egyptian taskmaster for beating his fellow descendent of Abraham. But this plan backfired. By the time he had arrived as a foreigner in the land of Midian, tending the flock of his father-in-law, it seems as though any fiery dream of leading his people to freedom had dimmed. He was, perhaps, jaded and contented with the fact that, if his people's God was planning to save them from their multigenerational plight, it would be by the hand of another.

I am, of course, describing Moses. Why this lengthy build up? Because it is important that we understand the kind of situation Moses found himself in when he first met the God of Israel. Since we come to this story as modern readers of a completed biblical canon, we may fail to be adequately surprised by the quantum leap that occurs in God's self-revelation in Exodus 3:14–15. After all, in this story, Moses learns that the name of his people's God is Yahweh—"He Is" (Ex. 3:15). This can seem rather unsurprising for us, who have—by the time we get to Exodus 3 in our Bibles—already read that name numerous times. When you read "LORD" in your Bible in small capital letters, you are reading an English substitution for Yahweh—"He Is." So when God introduces himself to Moses as "I AM" (Ex. 3:14), we are not struck by that significance because we are already well-acquainted with "I AM" doing things in the written narrative: It was "I AM" who created the first man from the dust of the earth (Gen. 2:7); it was "I AM" who flooded the earth, sparing Noah and his family (Gen. 6:5–8); it was "I AM" who called Abraham to leave his country (Gen. 12:1), blessed his son Isaac (Gen. 26:12), and visited Isaac's son Jacob in a dream (Gen. 28:10–22), and so on. But we have to remember, everything we read leading up to the story of Moses was written and collated by Moses himself under the inspiration of the Holy Spirit. The name—Yahweh, "He Is"—was reflected in those oral traditions through Moses's own pen many years after he had this encounter on Mount Horeb. The fruit of Moses's theological contemplation on *this* encounter would eventuate in the books of Genesis, Exodus, Leviticus, Numbers, and Deuteronomy. All this special revelation—all this divinely inspired text—did not precede Moses's encounter but would rather flow *from* it.

So to fully appreciate the monumental event in Exodus 3, we have to put ourselves in his sandals. Prior to this, Moses had stories and traditions and (possibly) fragmentary written accounts of the Deity of his people—who claims to have created everything—occasionally showing up and visiting his ancestors and making promises. That's not *no* information, but it's also not very much. Moses has no Bible to study, no religion to follow, no worship practices revealed and instituted to which he must adhere, no directions for prayer or intercession to apply, and no name to call this God.

With this minimal amount of information to work with, Moses discovered something striking: a bush engulfed in fire but not consumed by it (Ex. 3:2). With his curiosity aroused, Moses approached the bush and was thereby addressed by "the angel of the LORD" who commanded him to remove his sandals since the ground near this bush was "holy ground"

(Ex. 3:2–5). To stand in the presence of God is to stand on holy ground. "This place is not ordinary," God was essentially saying. "You can't walk around here as if it were. My holy presence is here; therefore, consecrate yourself and demonstrate your awareness of my unique majesty. Take your shoes off. Don't track the filth of your worldly dealings into this place."

At this point, God identified himself as the God of Moses's ancestors: "I am the God of your father, the God of Abraham, the God of Isaac, and the God of Jacob" (Ex. 3:6). Why is this significant? It's significant because it shows that God was weaving Moses into the story of redemption he had been writing since the events recorded in Genesis. God wanted Moses to know, in other words, that he was being brought into a divine story—he is a character within the same epic drama as Abraham, Isaac, and Jacob. Jacob, of course, was the father of the nation of Israel. The descendents of his twelve sons are the twelve tribes of Israel, all of which were—at the very moment of this conversation on Mount Horeb—in slavery to Egypt.

Now, we know that back in Genesis 15, God promised Abraham that his descendants would be "sojourners in a land that is not theirs and will be servants there, and they will be afflicted for four hundred years. But I will bring judgment on the nation that they serve, and afterward they shall come out with great possessions" (Gen. 15:13–14), which means that things are all going according to plan. Moses is being swept up into the story of his ancestors, which will one day result in the arrival of the Messiah, Jesus Christ.

Keep all that in mind when you read about God's response to his people's plight in Exodus 3:7–10:

> Then the LORD said, "I have surely seen the affliction of my people who are in Egypt and have heard their cry because of their taskmasters. I know their sufferings, and I have come down to deliver them out of the hand of the Egyptians and to bring them up out of that land to a good and broad land, a land flowing with milk and honey, to the place of the Canaanites, the Hittites, the Amorites, the Perizzites, the Hivites, and the Jebusites. And now, behold, the cry of the people of Israel has come to me, and I have also seen the oppression with which the Egyptians oppress them. Come, I will send you to Pharaoh that you may bring my people, the children of Israel, out of Egypt."

So God was recruiting Moses to be the instrument he would use to keep his promise to Abraham (cf. Gen. 15:18–21).

In Moses's response, we see the disposition that I described above. Whatever grandiose plans Moses may have had for his life before his exile to the land of Midian, he was probably deflated by the time he encountered the God of his ancestors on Mount Horeb. "But Moses said to God, 'Who am I that I should go to Pharaoh and bring the children of Israel out of Egypt?' He said, 'But I will be with you, and this shall be the sign for you, that I have sent you: when you have brought the people out of Egypt, you shall serve God on this mountain' "

(Ex. 3:11–12). Moses, intimidated by this lofty call, insisted that he was not the man for the job. God's consolation, in response, is a promise: I will be with you and bring you back to worship me again at this very mountain. In light of how fragmentary his knowledge and theology was at this point, the question for Moses is What makes this God's presence such a consolation, such a comfort? Who is he anyway? Basically, Moses needed some kind of assurance of success—some kind of revelation of this God's character.

> Then Moses said to God, "If I come to the people of Israel and say to them, 'The God of your fathers has sent me to you,' and they ask me, 'What is his name?' what shall I say to them?" God said to Moses, "I AM WHO I AM." And he said, "Say this to the people of Israel: 'I AM has sent me to you.'" God also said to Moses, "Say this to the people of Israel: 'The LORD, the God of your fathers, the God of Abraham, the God of Isaac, and the God of Jacob, has sent me to you.' This is my name forever, and thus I am to be remembered throughout all generations. (Ex. 3:13–15)

"I AM WHO I AM." *Yahweh*. This is the name God gives to Moses. It is the covenant name of the covenant-making, covenant-keeping God of Israel. And the name he gives simply is "HE *Is*."

What could this possibly mean? How is this even an answer? The answer to Moses's question is ultimately incomprehensible to him or to us: The personal name God gave is a disclosure of the kind of being he is—and the "kind" of being he *is*, is one who cannot be considered in relation to anything but *himself*. He is absolute Being. One theologian helpfully says, "Strictly speaking, God can only be understood by reference to God. . . . Exodus 3:14 jolts us by saying that God is not grouped with others. God can only be known by comparison to himself."[1] This cannot be said of any of us. We describe who we are *by* describing ourselves in categories of genus and species. We learn about ourselves specifically in relation to others. To learn about *me*, you learn about human beings in general, males more specifically, married men and fathers of young children even more specifically, and so on. We fit within categories and are comparable to like kinds within those categories. But God cannot name his essence by locating himself in a broad category that he fits within. He's not an object within the universe on which we can fit our attention. For God to be "I AM" means he is absolute, incomprehensible, unbounded *Being*.

He never became, nor is he becoming—he simply *is*. This sets him over against every other kind of being since every other kind of being derives its being from another. I am—because I was begotten by my parents in 1991. Before that, I didn't exist—I didn't have being. And even now, I don't own my being. I am—because I am receiving life (ultimately from

1 R. Michael Allen, "Exodus 3," in *Theological Commentary: Evangelical Perspectives*, ed. R. Michael Allen (T&T Clark, 2011), 32.

God but also from oxygen, food, water, sleep, etc.). I cannot declare myself independent from all else. But the God who spoke with Moses that day on Mount Horeb is utterly independent: He does not *receive* life, light, love, or being; he *is* light, life, love, and being. Everything else that exists, exists according to his will. He is not *becoming*—he *is*. Petrus van Mastricht, the great German-born seventeenth-century Reformed theologian, refered to aseity as "the highest and chief perfection of God," which "therefore must be located in the first place, because from it the rest of his perfections flow."[2]

But this is still positive revelation. In Exodus 3, God does not simply delete content from how we think about him; he's not simply telling us what he is by telling us what is *not* true of him. Rather, he truly does name himself *positively* when he puts this name on Moses's lips. He is, in other words, utterly sufficient in and of himself. He is, as the old theologians would say, the infinite plentitude of life, love, and holiness. And this means that he is perfect—in need of nothing and no one to make him more alive, more powerful, more happy, more knowledgeable.[3] Every other thing that exists gets all its life, power, happiness, and knowledge from him.

This means, practically, that God does not need us. God did not *need* Israel. He did not deliver the people by the hand of

2 Petrus van Mastricht, *Faith in the Triune God*, vol. 2 of *Theoretical-Practical Theology*, ed. Joel R. Beeke, trans. Todd M. Rester (Reformation Heritage, 2019), 90.

3 For this reason, the great theologians called God *pure act*.

Moses because he desired to somehow be enriched by their worship. The one who is—whose existence transcends all earthly consideration—is, by definition, everlastingly happy in himself. Later, we will see that this happiness burns in a uniquely Trinitarian way, but at this point I merely bring up this eternal self-happiness—or blessedness or beatitude—to disabuse us of the presumption that God's happiness depends on us.

Now, this may be a shock to those of us who are accustomed to flattering ourselves with certain contemporary praise songs or ill-considered children's Bibles, some of which can give the impression that God cannot be happy until heaven is populated by *us*. But this is simply not true. We don't make up for any deficiency in God. We don't fill an emotional hole in his heart. Our praise, although glorifying him and pleasing him in a sense, does not enrich him in his infinite joy. How could it? All the praise we offer—all the good we render to him—originates from him (cf. 1 Chron. 29:14; 1 Cor. 4:7). "For from him," says Paul, "and through him and to him are all things" (Rom. 11:36). He who is infinite in his perfection is, therefore, infinite in his blessedness and, therefore, cannot be enriched by another in any way.

Just consider how Herman Bavinck portrays this doctrine:

> By this perfection he is at once essentially and absolutely distinct from all creatures. Creatures, after all, do not derive their existence from themselves but from others and so have

> nothing from themselves; both in their origin and hence in their further development and life, they are absolutely dependent. But . . . God is exclusively from himself, not in the sense of being self-caused but being from eternity to eternity who he is, being, not becoming. God is absolute being, the fullness of being, and therefore also eternally and absolutely independent in his existence, in his perfections, in all his works, the first and the last, the sole cause and final goal of all things. In this aseity of God, conceived not only as having being from himself but also as the fullness of being, all the other perfections are included.[4]

This is a marvelous truth. Why? Why should we be pleased when God disabuses us of our self-flattering perspective that we benefit him? Because if God does not need us, then he has created and redeemed us out of his pure, undiluted, gratuitous, unconstrained, and noncompulsory love.

Question: If God does not need us and is not enriched by us, why then does he create and redeem us? Answer: Simply out of a free expression of his infinitely overflowing love! This means that the love of God manifested in creating and redeeming his people is preeminently trustworthy. Since its foundation and goal is a creaturely participation in God's own eternal beatitude, nothing creaturely can alter it. If the source

4 Herman Bavinck, *God and Creation*, vol. 2 of *Reformed Dogmatics*, ed. John Bolt, trans. John Vriend (Baker Academic, 2004), 152.

of our eternal life is the *a se* eternal love of God, then we can bank all our security on it.

Do you see how this might be a consolation to Moses? "How will this God's presence help me?" Moses may have asked himself. "Who is this one who will be with me as I go to Pharoah?" Answer: *the one who is*. He *is* the infinite source and giver of all life and being. Moses could not appeal categorically higher than to this Being for help in his task to deliver Israel from slavery. Who could help Moses more on this mission? Sure, Pharoah was the king of the greatest earthly superpower—Moses had seen that up close. Sure, no living man was more powerful than he. Sure, Moses was a jaded, humiliated, failed deliverer coming to this people with a deficit of credibility to lead them. But the Being who commissioned Moses in Exodus 3 is the one who gives life and breath and being to everyone, including Pharoah. Moses had the help of the infinite Maker of heaven and earth behind him: He should almost feel bad for Pharoah! No competition against "I AM" is even fair.

So we can derive the doctrine of aseity from the Scriptures in several ways. We can discern it in God's creation of the cosmos from nothing—that is, God is independent of the created world because his being precedes, transcends, and causes the created world by definition. Or we can derive the doctrine of aseity by contrasting God to other gods—that is, God differs from idols precisely in the sense that they depend on their worshipers while God does not depend on us. But the passage we have considered in this chapter arrives at the doctrine in a manner a bit more on the nose. In Exodus 3 we learn that God positively teaches us of his aseity, simply by naming himself as he who is who he is. The God of the Christian Scriptures, alone, *is*.

4

In the Beginning Was the Word

WHEN YOU READ the first words in the Bible, "In the beginning, God created the heavens and the earth" (Gen. 1:1), you can place a massive mental wedge between those two words "God" and "created." On the left side, you have the Creator: God. On the right, you have creation: everything else, all that is not God. This, as we noted previously, implies our doctrine of divine aseity. Nothing on the right side of this Creator-creature divide can in any way define what is on the left side. One of the ways we identify who's who in this scheme is to ask the questions, Which one doesn't need the other, and which is defined by its need of the other? We cannot come to imagine the Creator and the creature in a mutually defining way without either making God out to be a creature, on the one hand, or making creation out to be God, on the other. So the first verse of the Bible tells us about divine aseity indirectly, by pure negation. At least part of what it means for God to be God is for him to *not* be creation, which means that unlike creation, God is independent. But does the New Testament add any texture to this understanding of divine aseity? Yes. Quite a bit actually.

Imagine, as a thought experiment, sitting down with the apostle John, the beloved disciple, after he's written the first draft of his Gospel. Let's say you're invited to hear him recite it aloud and to offer your feedback. Let's also pretend that you are a well-read, first-century Jew who knows little of Jesus but who knows the Jewish Scriptures well, having been steeped in them from your youth. Also, since (as was the case for first-century Jews) you have grown up within the context of the Roman Empire and have been enculturated in a thoroughly Greek environment, you have some working knowledge of Greek philosophy and its technical terminology. So there you are, sitting in a room with John who holds an open scroll before you. He clears his throat and begins to read: "In the beginning." He pauses for effect, long enough to allow you to complete the phrase in your mind: *God created the heavens and the earth*. And you wonder, *I thought John was reading something* he *wrote. Why is he quoting Moses's words?* No sooner do you ask yourself this, however, than John utterly surprises you by changing the words: ". . . was the *Word*, and the Word was *with* God, and the Word *was God*" (John 1:1). Just as the opening salvo of Genesis contains galaxies of theological implications, so too do the opening words of John's Gospel, which intentionally converses with Genesis 1:1.

This slight shift of the Genesis account would remind you—a Jew who knows the Jewish Scriptures—of all the ways Yahweh's *word* is talked about and personified in the Old Testament. You would think about Psalm 33:6:

> By the *word* of the LORD the heavens were made,
> and by the *breath* of his mouth all their host.

You would also recall Yahweh's promise through Isaiah that his word would go out and accomplish his purposes (Isa. 55:10–11). These thoughts would be reinforced as John continues to read: "He was in the beginning with God. All things were made through him, and without him was not anything made that was made" (John 1:2–3). At this point, your mind would probably rummage through Proverbs and rest on the description of wisdom in Proverbs 8—personified as a preexistent agent alongside Yahweh, establishing Yahweh's creation (see Prov. 8:22–31).

And as a Jew whose entire culture had been, since before you were born, thoroughly Hellenized (that is, influenced by the Greek culture of the Roman Empire that governed your people), you would also find it striking that John uses the Greek word *logos* ("Word"). It would conjure up all sorts of connotations about *reason* as the underlying structure of the universe—the most fundamental organizing principle that governs all things and the integrating point that ultimately connects any one part of the cosmos to any other. According to some from the Greek philosophical tradition, at the very foundation of the cosmos is eternal, transcendent reason. And this, too, would seem to make sense of what John's Gospel is saying.

And the most striking detail—the one undeniable feature that would shock you like a bucket of cold water emptied on your unsuspecting head—is that this Word is clearly not being portrayed as an attribute of God, nor a product of God's creative ingenuity, nor merely a power or ability that God possesses. Rather, in your ears, John describes this Word as somehow *personally distinct* from God while also truly being *God himself*. This would be utterly stunning to you, as a first-time hearer of this Gospel, especially in light of your Jewish upbringing. Despite the fact that the Jewish people had assimilated to Roman culture in many ways and lived in a Hellenized Palestine, you are proud that your people could never abide Rome's pantheon of gods. No matter how Hellenized you may have become, your people would never accept the polytheism of your overlords. To be a Jew was to believe in one God alone—to be a monotheist. What you would find so surprising about John's Gospel is that John was in no way walking back his Jewish roots in this respect. The inclusion of this personal Word within the Godhead (and, as you would eventually discover while John continued to read his Gospel aloud, the inclusion of another person—the Spirit) was not expressed as a departure from the Scriptures of your ancestors. John was portraying Yahweh in a manner totally consistent with the monotheistic portrait of Jewish Scripture, even while bringing something truly new to one's understanding of God.

I have taken you through this thought experiment to highlight the shocking but crucial truth of God's New Testament self-revelation in the coming of Christ and the Spirit: The timelessly eternal and *a se* God of the Old Testament is *triune*. God did not become triune with the coming of the Son at Advent and the coming of the Spirit at Pentecost. If Exodus 3:14 tells us that the God of Christian Scripture *is*, the New Testament tells us that this same God who *is*, is the God who *is Trinity*.

Consider again that mental wedge we placed between "God" and "created" in Genesis 1:1. This wedge—this Creator-creature distinction—was a necessary principle in John's thinking as well, and it becomes very instructive for us as we try to parse out his language. John agrees that there is one being alone who exists on the left side of this wedge: Yahweh, the Creator God of Scripture. And yet, John places a person who is both *distinct* from Israel's God ("the Word was *with* God") and *is* the "I AM" of the Old Testament ("and the Word was God") over on the God side of this divide. Genesis 1 teaches that God alone creates what is not God, and John 1 teaches that God never creates what is not God without his Word. This precludes us from putting the Word on the right side of this wedge. If all that is not God is made by the Word, then the Word cannot exist on the "not God" side of the Creator-creature divide (John 1:3).

"He was in the beginning with God," John tells us (John 1:2), which means that he exists in the timeless eternity of God's self-existence. So when we read, "In the beginning, *God,*" John is telling us that the Word was there with him.

This principle comes home even more significantly as we continue to read: "In him was life" (John 1:4). Unlike creation, the Word did not *derive* his life from God. In him—while he was "in the beginning" with God—*was* life. Rather than making the Word the finite recipient of life from the underived life of God, John makes him out to be the giver of all life and light to the world: "In him was life, and the life was the light of men" (John 1:4).

The miracle of the incarnation is that this divine life—this light of men, this Word of God—came into the world *as* man (John 1:9–11). "The Word became flesh and dwelt among us," says John, "and we have seen his glory, glory as of the only Son from the Father, full of grace and truth" (John 1:14). In other words, John has something new to teach us because this God who created the cosmos out of nothing and revealed himself to Moses as "I AM" has revealed himself in a new and surprising way at the incarnation. The Word of God came *as* man to be the Word of God *to* man—he came to exegete, to reveal, to disclose the divine nature more fully. And this act of revelation—this self-disclosure of triune preexistence—was intrinsically saving. "I AM" saves as he reveals, and he reveals as he saves. "From his fullness," John says, "we have all received, grace upon grace" (John 1:16). In other words, from the plentitude of independent life—from he who has life in and of himself—we receive life. And this reception is grace upon grace: grace in giving us life as creatures (John 1:3), grace in giving us the instruction of the law through Moses (John 1:17), and the grace of everlasting life in being incorporated into the family of God (John 1:12–13).

"No one has ever seen God; the only God, who is at the Father's side, he has made him known" (John 1:18). Jesus, in saving us, reveals God to us. He makes known the unknowable God as the image of the invisible (Col. 1:15). He is the light of God (Heb. 1:1–3), who reveals him who dwells in unapproachable light (1 Tim. 6:16). Jesus can do these things because—and only because—he, as the Word, is preexistent Being: the "I AM."

Later, we will consider the relationship between the Word being life and our reception of life through him (cf. John 1:9–13; 1:16). For now I want to emphasize that this Word is not a beneficiary of life like the rest of creation; he is, rather, the benefactor of life. He gives from his "fullness," his plentitude, the overflowing and effulgent wellspring of his very being. Christ cannot give by grace what he does not have by nature. He grants eternal life because eternal life is his to give. He shows the glory of the Father because the glory of the Father is his to show.

We could go on reflecting on the Son's divinity—the fact that he belongs on the Creator side of the Creator-creature divide—but my point is not merely to make the case that the doctrine of the Trinity is biblical. Rather, I mean to draw your attention to the fact that the doctrine of the Trinity—particularly as it is revealed in the prologue of John's Gospel—enriches our understanding of the doctrine of aseity. It is not merely that "the God who is" happens to be Trinity but, rather, that God's aseity—God's being *of himself*—is a triune aseity. Given this, it remains to be shown how the endlessly blazing fire of divine aseity burns *as* Father, Son, and Spirit. What does John's Gospel teach us about the divine life of the divine persons in their relations to each other? We shall consider these matters next.

5

Only Begotten God

ORDINARILY, IT IS NOT ADVISABLE to quibble with Bible translations. Many Christians know that there are a range of translations available—some tending to be more accurate than others. Some are less translations than they are paraphrases. But for the most part, a Bible translation that receives any level of widespread acceptance has probably done so for good reasons. Typically, Bible translations are the fruit of a lengthy process undertaken by a large team of highly qualified and specialized scholars who have devoted the better parts of their lives to mastering biblical languages and the skill of translation. This means that the average reader, who has no intention of learning Greek, Hebrew, or Aramaic, does not have to fear missing some essential teaching when he approaches his Bible. Of course, learning how to read in these languages can surely enrich one's understanding. Pastors and scholars would do well to exercise the discipline and devotion to their teaching task by studying the biblical languages. But those who simply read most English translations of the Bible can rest assured that they are reading a trustworthy rendering of what God and his human authors intended to communicate.

And yet, I think most modern translations have room for improvement in the Gospel of John with respect to one specific word. The Greek word is *monogenēs*, and it is often translated as "only," "one and only," or "unique." John uses this word four times in his Gospel (John 1:14, 18; 3:16, 18). In most ways, modern translations are preferable to older ones not only because they communicate ancient truths to modern-day readers in a language they can better understand but also because their source material for translation work is substantially larger and more dependable than older translations—like the King James Version. But on *this* word, I think the King James Version has most of its contemporary competitors beat. A better translation of *monogenēs* in John's Gospel, the one the KJV uses, is not merely "only" or "unique" but, rather, "only begotten":

> And the Word was made flesh, and dwelt among us, (and we beheld his glory, the glory as of the *only begotten* of the Father,) full of grace and truth. (John 1:14 KJV)

> No man hath seen God at any time; the *only begotten Son*, which is in the bosom of the Father, he hath declared him. (John 1:18 KJV)

> For God so loved the world, that he gave his *only begotten* Son, that whosoever believeth in him should not perish, but have everlasting life. (John 3:16 KJV)

> He that believeth on him is not condemned: but he that believeth not is condemned already, because he hath not believed in the name of the *only begotten* Son of God. (John 3:18 KJV)

My point is not to adjudicate academic debates among Greek scholars—I couldn't improve on the work of those who have already done this.[1] My point, rather, is to explain why the doctrine I'm about to introduce might feel unfamiliar and even, at first glance, unintuitive. The doctrine is called *eternal generation*, or *eternal begottenness,* and it refers to the way the Son relates to the Father within the Godhead. It may *feel* unfamiliar or foreign to the Scriptures, but that's because you aren't reading "only *begotten*" in these key passages. Now, I intend to show that this doctrine does not rise or fall with the translation of this single word; nevertheless, failing to use this language of "only begotten Son" does put the contemporary reader at a disadvantage when considering this topic. The foregoing discussion on translation is merely my attempt to even the odds. This *is* a biblical doctrine. Not

1 See Charles Lee Irons, "A Lexical Defense of the Johannine 'Only Begotten,'" in *Retrieving Eternal Generation*, ed. Fred Sanders and Scott R. Swain (Zondervan Academic, 2017).

only that, it is also a biblical doctrine that has unimaginably significant ramifications on our theology and, in particular, on our conception of divine aseity. Eternal generation is at the heart of what it means for Christians to confess faith in the *Trinity*. And, as we will see in subsequent chapters, this has everything to do with a *Christian* portrayal of divine aseity: Our God is *a se* because he is infinitely full not merely in divine happiness but in *triune* bliss.

So what does eternal generation mean? It describes the manner in which the Father and the Son relate in the timeless eternity of the simple being of God—that is, it affirms that the Son relates to the Father as eternally generated or eternally begotten from the Father. The Father generates; the Son is generated. The Father begets; the Son is begotten.

Now, I understand that this may raise more questions than we started with. It may appear as though I have tried to clarify a misty phrase with an even mistier definition, adding confusion to confusion. Perhaps I can begin to dispel some of the fog by explaining what is meant by "begotten." While it is not a word we use in common parlance, it is useful to distinguish between different kinds of relationships. My son—whose philosophical quandary about God's eternal life sparked this reflection in chapter 1—is my begotten. I begat him. As it turns out, he looks very much like me, but that is not what renders him my begotten. If, for example, I were able to create a wax sculpture of myself to capture an identical likeness, it would look even more like me than my son, but it would not be my begotten. I also happen to love my son quite a lot, but that does not render him my begotten either. Were I ever to purchase a pet dog, I'm sure I would grow to love it, but my love for it would not transform it into my begotten. No, my son is my begotten because he was generated by me—he is my offspring. That is why he is called my son and why I am called his father. This relation is what we call *ontological*. When I say that I have begotten a son, you may not know anything about him personally, but you know at least two things about him: He is human, and he derived his humanity, in part, from my humanity.

To highlight that first truth, we know intuitively that like begets like. People beget people; dogs beget dogs; cats beget cats. That which is begotten shares in the same essence as that which it begets. I may call a dog my "child," but you know I cannot mean that literally, since humans don't beget dogs. In an analogous way, the doctrine of eternal generation affirms that what the Father is, the Son is also. What God begets is God. Eternal generation, in other words, affirms the full divinity of the Son. As we observed in the previous chapter, the Son belongs on the Creator side of the Creator-creature divide.

But there's more. As I said, if I tell you that I have begotten a son, you know that he is human, but you also know that he is a human from my humanity. In other words, my son and I don't relate to one another in the same way that I relate to you. No, my begotten is a human whose relation to me is unique in the sense that he derived his humanity from my humanity, and this part of our relation is one directional. He derives his humanity from mine, but I don't derive mine from his. Similarly, the doctrine of eternal generation not only affirms that the Son is divine just as the Father is but also that the Son is generated *from* the Father. There is a directionality that is never reversed: The Father is ungenerate, and the Son is generate; the Son is *from* the Father, the Father is not *from* the Son. So eternal generation teaches that the Son is *what* the Father is (namely, divine) and that the Son is *what* the Father is *from the Father*.

Now, when we speak about God with analogy—as *all* speech from finite creatures about an infinite God is—we necessarily embrace similarity and dissimilarity. An analogy is both like and unlike the thing we are trying to describe. Up until now, our reflections on eternal generation have focused on the similarity implicit with this word "generation." The Father's generation of the Son is like my generation of my son. But divine generation is also radically unlike human generation. We can get at the dissimilarity by calling attention to the other word in the doctrine's name: "eternal." My begetting of my son is, like everything about my finite existence, time bound. There was a time when I was not a father—I became a father. But the Father's generation of the Son is eternal—it never began, and it will never end. The Father is eternally Father of his Son. Likewise, the Son was never brought into existence by his Father—he is the eternally begotten Son. And the Spirit—as we will discuss in due course—is breathed out and given as the love of the Father and the Son. But his being breathed out never began. He is the timelessly eternal love of the Father and the Son. Never was there a time when the Father was without his Son and Spirit, and never was the Son without his Spirit and Father. Never was the divine Lord without his Word and his love.

All of this reminds us that we should never be tempted to attribute differing degrees of glory, might, or authority to the Father, Son, or Spirit. The Son and the Spirit are not the result of the Father's will, as if he decided one day that he was lonely and wanted to have a Son. No, rather, he ever lives to beget the Son and breathe out the Spirit. To be the Father is to be the Father of the Son. There is no Father without eternal generation and eternal spiration (the name we give for the Spirit's procession from the Father and Son—his being "breathed out" eternally by them), so there is no Father without the Son and Spirit. All that the Father is, is begotten as the Son; and all that the Father and Son are, is breathed out as the Spirit. This includes the divine will, the divine majesty, the divine glory—indeed, the divine nature. That means that the divine will is always the will of Father, Son, and Spirit. The divine glory is the divine glory of Father, Son, and Spirit. And this is because on the left side of that Creator-creature divide, there is only one Being, and that Being is a consuming fire of life and light and love that ever burns in this way: as Father, Son, and Spirit.

This is why the Nicene Creed uses the language that it uses:

> And [I believe] in one Lord Jesus Christ, the only-
>   begotten Son of God,
>   begotten of the Father before all worlds;

> God of God, Light of Light, very God of very God;
> begotten, not made, being of one substance with the Father,
> by whom all things were made.[2]

Where is the doctrine of eternal generation? Shining like a blazing sun in every "of" in that statement: "Son *of* God," "begotten *of* the Father," "God *of* God," "Light *of* Light," "very God *of* very God."

And of the Spirit, the creed confesses,

> And I believe in the Holy Spirit, the Lord and Giver of life;
> who proceeds *from* the Father and the Son;
> who *with* the Father and the Son together is worshiped and glorified.[3]

Since the Spirit proceeds eternally from the Father and the Son, he is worshiped and glorified together with the Father and the Son. The latter portion of the creed follows from the former. And this confession to worship the Spirit with the Father and the Son can be understood as both a kind of imperative and a kind of indicative—something we *ought* to do and something that simply *is done.* On the one hand, since the Spirit proceeds from the Father and the Son, we ought not

2 "The Nicene Creed," in *Creeds, Confessions, and Catechisms: A Reader's Edition*, ed. Chad Van Dixhoorn (Crossway, 2022), 17.

3 "The Nicene Creed," 17–18.

neglect worshiping the Spirit. All that God is, the Spirit is, since all that God is, is from the Father *to* the Son and *in* the Spirit. But considered from another angle, the Spirit's irreducible procession from the Father and the Son means that he simply is worshiped and glorified whenever the Father and the Son are truly worshiped. To worship the Father is to worship the Father of the eternal Son and Spirit—one does not receive glory apart from the other two. Their "glory equal, the majesty coeternal," as the Athanasian Creed says.[4]

What does all of this have to do with the doctrine of aseity? Everything! Remember, the doctrine of aseity, negatively stated, simply affirms that God is independent—God exists in and of himself. God needs nothing. But the doctrine of aseity positively stated affirms that the reason God needs nothing is that he is the plentitude of life and blessedness. He is the infinitely bursting forth reservoir of happiness that never stops pouring and never diminishes. His delight and contentment cannot wane because they are boundlessly radiant. Well, the doctrine of the Trinity—and in particular, eternal generation—helps us see *how* this fire burns, how this fountain pours, how this light radiates. The doctrine of the Trinity is what makes the happy doctrine of aseity happy. To be God is to be infinite love—love of Father for Son, love of Son for Father, Spirit as love from Father and Son.

4 "The Athanasian Creed," in Van Dixhoorn, *Creeds, Confessions, and Catechisms*, 21.

All of this grants us a greater depth of appreciation for God's attributes—divine aseity in particular. For example, as the great theologians of the past would say, God is not a combination of act and potential to act. Rather, he is pure act. To say that God is pure act is to deny to him any capacity for change—either of improvement or diminishment. As creatures who are fundamentally finite and therefore fundamentally changing and changeable, we are entirely a combination of *potential* and *act*. Who I am at the very moment I write this sentence in the year of our Lord 2024 (act) is the realization of potential I have had ever since—and before—my birth in 1991 (potential). The potential I had back then has been actualized by many contributing factors that have brought me from there to here. We are never pure potential, nor pure act, but always and at every moment a combination of act and potency. But God has no potential—God is only act, pure and simple. The doctrine of the Trinity helps us understand, even dimly, why *pure act* is not a boring, lifeless affirmation—like the florescent lights of an office accidently left on overnight. The life of God is infinitely dynamic and vivacious: The being of God *is* the eternal Father eternally begetting his Son, and the eternal Father and Son eternally breathing out their Spirit.

At this point you may ask, What makes us so sure that this is in fact how God is? Demonstrating that this vision of Trinitarian theology is found in the Nicene Creed is simple enough. But is it supported by Scripture, or is it a later invention? The test of genuineness, of course, can only be decided by reading Scripture itself. In other words, we might ask, Do these affirmations bring clarity to the Scripture, or do they obscure its meaning? This is a fair question, and we will continue to look to John's Gospel for guidance in answering it.

6

Come and See

IN HIS CLASSIC epic poem *The Divine Comedy*, Dante Alighieri narrates an imaginative journey from hell to heaven. His travels begin with a descent through the nine circles of hell (part I, the *Inferno*). Having passed through to the other side, he begins a trek up the mountain of purgatory (part II, the *Purgatorio*). From there he will be lifted up in the heavens, passing through heavenly realm after heavenly realm to eventually come into the presence of the triune God in paradise (part III, the *Paradiso*). The *Divine Comedy* is a rich and overwhelming masterpiece that pulls together insights from the entire Western theological tradition preceding Dante, as well as the most striking insights from history and mythology. Throughout his journey, Dante relies on a couple of guides. His first usher, who takes him through hell and most of the way up the mount of purgatory, is Virgil—the great Roman poet and author of the *Aeneid*. Before reaching the top of purgatory's mount, however, Virgil passes Dante to the guiding care of Dante's beloved muse, Beatrice. She takes Dante nearly all the way through heaven into the presence of the Trinity. Profound lessons abound in the *Divine Comedy* on sin, sanctification, theology proper, and the Christian life, and it is no wonder that it is considered an unrivaled work in the Western tradition.

We who have been contemplating the doctrine of divine aseity—and in particular, aseity in its Trinitarian dimensions—find ourselves now in a place of desperate need not unlike the situation Dante found himself in at the start of his *Divine Comedy*. Dante captures our mood in his plea with Virgil:

> Lead me this way. Beyond this present ill
> and worse to dread, lead me to Peter's gate
> and be my guide.[1]

We, too, need a guide to help us navigate these dizzying heights as we contemplate divine aseity. Our journey now comes to the life and ministry of Jesus, so we shall let John the beloved disciple continue to lead us along the contours of his Gospel. Why John's Gospel? To answer this question, we might solicit

1 Dante Alighieri, *The Inferno*, in *The Divine Comedy*, trans. John Ciardi (New American Library, 2003), 1.124–26.

the help of another poet—this time a modern one—Malcolm Guite. Consider this sonnet Guite wrote about the Gospel of John:

> This is the Gospel of the primal light,
> The first beginning, and fruitful end,
> The soaring glory of an eagle's flight,
> The quiet touch of a beloved friend.
> This is the Gospel of our transformation,
> Water to wine and grain to living bread,
> Blindness to sight and sorrow to elation,
> And Lazarus himself back from the dead!
> This is the Gospel of all inner meaning,
> The heart of heaven opened to the earth,
> A gentle friend on Jesus' bosom leaning,
> And Nicodemus offered a new birth.
> No need to search the heavens high above,
> Come close with John, and feel the pulse of Love.[2]

This poem is rife with opportunities to reflect on John's Gospel for spiritual nourishment, and we could analyze each line for the rest of this little book. But suffice it to say, Guite gives us as good a reason as any to let John be our guide as we consider the doctrine of divine aseity through the life and ministry of Jesus.

2 Malcolm Guite, *Sounding the Seasons: Seventy Sonnets for the Church Year* (Canterbury, 2012), 6. Reproduced with permission of the Licensor through PLSclear.

"No need to search the heavens high above." Why? Because heaven has come in the person of Christ, and John introduces us to him in all his heavenly grandeur. So we heed Guite's advice: "Come close with John, and feel the pulse of Love."

Following our rapid plunge into the whitewaters of Nicene Trinitarianism in the previous chapter, I posed a question: What makes us so sure that this is in fact how God is? I suggested that the test of genuineness would come from putting these Nicene categories to work in our reading of the Scriptures. Do these categories make sense of what Scripture confronts us with, or do they obscure what we find there? Let us ask our guide. Let us inquire of John if these lessons on eternal generation and the aseity of the Trinity make sense of the life of Christ. Are we on solid ground, John?

"Come and see," he replies through the lips of Philip (John 1:46). So we come near with Nathanael, and we are startled as he shouts his own conclusion, "Rabbi, you are the Son of God! You are the King of Israel!" (John 1:49). Jesus replies, "Truly, truly, I say to you, you will see heaven opened, and the angels of God ascending and descending on the Son of Man" (John 1:51). In speaking this way, Jesus refers to an episode that would have been committed to memory as sacrosanct in the mind of every pious Jew: Jacob's dream of a ladder to heaven (Gen 28:10–22). "This is none other than the house of God," Jacob said, "and this is the gate to heaven" (Gen 28:17). In making himself the place where angels ascend and descend, Jesus self-identifies as "the gate to heaven." This is not the last time he will do this in John's Gospel, of course (cf. John 10:7), nor is it the only time that he is talked about in this way. To recognize Christ as the "gate to heaven," as the meeting place between heaven and earth—between Creator and creature—is simply another way of affirming that the Word (who "was God," John 1:1) "became flesh and dwelt [or "tabernacled"] among us, and we have seen his glory, glory as of the only Son from the Father, full of grace and truth" (John 1:14). Therefore, when we heed Philip's invitation to "come and see," we learn—with Nathanael—a hermeneutical insight. Jesus's identity as the "gate to heaven" teaches us how to read his words when we encounter them in the Gospel.

On the one hand, Jesus can bring heaven to us because he is

> God of God, Light of Light, very God of very God;
> begotten, not made, being of one substance with the
> Father.[3]

When Jesus identifies himself as Jacob's ladder, it is not a presumption—he is not committing the hubris of Babel (cf. Gen 11:4) because he is not trying to climb up *to* heaven but has rather come down *from* heaven. He cannot bring what he does not have—he cannot lead to where he does not originate. The sphere of God's heavenly being can be found

3 "The Nicene Creed," in *Creeds, Confessions, and Catechisms: A Reader's Edition*, ed. Chad Van Dixhoorn (Crossway, 2022), 17.

in him because that is his sphere. On the other hand, he is Jacob's ladder touching solid ground. In other words, earth meets heaven in him, because not only was he "begotten of the Father before all worlds," but he also

> for us men and for our salvation,
> came down from heaven
> and was incarnate by the Holy Spirit and the
> Virgin Mary
> and was made man.[4]

Or as the Chalcedonian Definition articulates it, he is "begotten before the ages from the Father as regards his divinity, and in the last days the same for us and for our salvation from Mary, the virgin God-bearer, as regards his humanity."[5]

Jesus as the "gate to heaven"—the union of Creator and creature—means that we should expect to see both realities expressed in the narrative of Christ's life in a mysterious, otherworldly, paradoxical dance. But because this Christ is one, we should expect to see harmony between his earthly actions and his eternal relation to the Father and Spirit. In other words, while Jesus's life and ministry are the life and ministry of a man, they are the life and ministry of a person who is also—in a transcendent register—divine, bearing an eternal

4 "The Nicene Creed," 17.

5 "The Chalcedonian Definition," in Van Dixhoorn, *Creeds, Confessions, and Catechisms*, 27.

relation to the Father and the Spirit. His creaturely actions, words, and descriptions cannot be thoughtlessly conflated with his divine identity (lest we be tempted to suggest that the divine nature can sleep, grow, change, and die, since Jesus clearly did all these things in his humanity). But his creaturely actions, words, and descriptions nevertheless always reflect his divine identity. Let us, therefore, follow John as he continues to lead us in our contemplations.

Where is he leading us now? To a dark meeting place under the cover of night, where Christ converses with a Jewish leader. He shows us in his interaction with Nicodemus that he is the "only [begotten] Son," whom the Father gave as an expression of love, "that whoever believes in him should not perish but have eternal life" (John 3:16). This giving is also a sending (John 3:17), and the directionality here is key: The Father *gives* and *sends* the Son, not the other way around. And yet, lest we imagine that this means that the Son is somehow less than the Father, we are told that those who come to the Son in belief will thereby "have eternal life" (John 3:16). Which is to say, eternal life—which can only be given by God—is found in the Son who was given. Is this not because the divine life ever flows *from* the Father who is unbegotten and *through* the Son who is eternally begotten?

But our guide does not wish for us to linger on this episode for too long. John leads us now to a well just outside of Samaria, in the heat of the day, where we find Jesus conversing with a woman of ill repute. "Whoever drinks of the water that

I will give him," we overhear him saying to her, "will never be thirsty again. The water that I will give him will become in him a spring of water welling up to eternal life" (John 4:14). Again, we see Jesus offering to give what he has no authority to give *unless* he is divine. Of course, we will learn later that this water is given in the giving of the Spirit: "Whoever believes in me," says Jesus, "as the Scripture has said, 'Out of his heart will flow rivers of living water' " (John 7:38). John, the faithful guide that he is, provides a clarification on this point: "Now this he said about the Spirit, whom those who believed in him were to receive, for as yet the Spirit had not been given, because Jesus was not yet glorified" (John 7:39). So, at this well near Samaria, Jesus offers to give the woman the life-giving water of the Spirit's indwelling—a gift that wells up into overflowing streams of eternal life. Could he offer this life if it were not his to give? Could he offer to pour out the Spirit if the Spirit did not proceed from him?

Of course, John is not yet finished showing us what Jesus's ministry teaches about the *a se* life of God. Throughout his Gospel, John calls attention to the fact that Jesus had a habit of eliciting the accusation of blasphemy from some of his listeners. One particular example stands out as relevant for our present concerns. We see Jesus arouse the frustration of his opponents by healing a man on the Sabbath (John 5:1–8). In their estimation, Jesus has broken the fourth commandment (cf. Ex. 20:8–11). In response, Jesus reasons straightforwardly: "My Father is working until now, and I am working"

(John 5:17). In other words, "If the Father is allowed to continue to work on this day, so am I." At this point, John directs his attention to his readers to interpret the heated interaction: "This is why the Jews were seeking all the more to kill him, because not only was he breaking the Sabbath, but he was even calling God his own Father, making himself equal with God" (John 5:18).

At this point, Jesus is faced with a clear option. If he did not intend to communicate equality and shared authority with the Father, he could easily say so to deescalate the situation. "You misunderstand me," he could say, "I'm not saying I am equal to the Father. I'm just saying that God is probably fine with my doing this good work on the Sabbath." But he doesn't do this. Instead, Jesus doubles down on his statement and makes the starkness of his claim even more emphatic. "Truly, truly, I say to you, the Son can do nothing of his own accord, but only what he sees the Father doing" (John 5:19). Now, one way to interpret this statement is to distance his authority from the Father's, as if to say, "Don't shoot the messenger; I'm only following orders." But the following sentence makes that interpretation impossible: "For *whatever the Father* does, that the Son does likewise" (John 5:19). Notice, there is no daylight between the things the Father does and the things the Son does. Jesus is not saying that he does the kinds of things the Father does; rather, he says that the very things the Father does, the Son does likewise. What might these things include? Jesus tells us: raising the dead to life (John 5:21, 24, 25, 29) and receiving honor (John 5:23–24). According to Jesus, there is no honoring the Father without honoring the Son. Which is to say, Jesus claims that the divine act of raising the dead is carried out both by the Father and the Son; therefore, the Father and the Son receive the same honor. Even the act of divine judgment is a shared act between the Father and the Son—given from the Father, exercised by the Son (John 5:27).

But we have not quite seen enough. John would have us look even closer. Even while the execution of divine actions are attributed equally and identically to the Father and the Son in this passage, this does not mean that the persons, in carrying out these divine actions, are not distinguished from one another. On the one hand, the action of raising the dead—or giving life—is a single action that is attributed to both Father and Son. So the very action carried out by the Father and Son is identically singular. And it should be if they have the one divine essence and will in common. But, on the other hand, in carrying out the selfsame action, the Father and Son are distinguished from one another. There is a directionality here in these words. The Father *gives* judgment to the Son; the Father *gives* the Son to raise the dead at the sound of his voice. Does this simply mean that the Son is the Father's lacky? Not at all. In this passage, Jesus gives us the theological grounding of all this doing, giving, raising, and judging, and it provides us with breath-catching insight: "For as the Father has life in himself, so he has granted the Son also to have life in himself" (John 5:26).

The grammar of this single verse is all important. John, our mountaineer and guide, has just taken us—in our utter surprise—to the mountaintop of Christological contemplation. He has placed a window right here in the middle of the very ordinary house of human words to peer into the cathedral of the divine life. Jesus is *not* talking about God in relation to his creation. He is, rather, talking about the Father in eternal relation to his Son—that is, the inner life of the divine Godhead. How do we know this? Jesus himself makes this clear: "For as the Father has life *in himself*." This, beloved reader, is the doctrine we have been considering throughout this book. We would not be far off to rephrase these words in this way: "For as the Father has *aseity*." Jesus makes a statement about what it means for God to be God—he is making a statement about the inner life of God, that mysterious and dreadful topic that resists creaturely prying. How can we even deign to think about such depths? We do so humbly, with fear and trembling, because while it is terrifying to wade into the treacherously deep waters of Trinitarian theology, refusing to listen to our Lord is a far more treacherous prospect. "For as the Father has life *in himself*," he says, "so he has granted the Son also to have life in himself" (John 5:26).

He does not say, "as the Father has life in himself, so he has granted the Son to have *life*." Had he said this, he would have been saying something altogether uncontroversial. The *a se* God, who has life in himself, gives life to everyone. But that's not what Jesus says. Christ's words keep "the Son" on the *divine* side of the Creator-creature divide in the sense that he has aseity attributed to him: The Son has "life in himself." But this "life in himself" is given.

When did this happen? Well, there is no "when"! The Son has life as the Father has life—that is, in himself. Aseity, you see is an attribute that the Son has, along with the Father, because the divine nature is *a se*. And yet, Jesus says that the Son's being *a se* is "given" from the Father. The inner life of God, it would seem, is ever *from* the Father and "given" to the Son. Eternally, the Father *gives* life to the Son. And, to zoom back out to the passage at hand, this theological reality is the reason why all the Son's divine activity—which he shares with the Father—is *given* by the Father. Thus, this mono-directionality within the eternal life of God is echoed in creaturely revelation in time. Because the divine *a se* life is from the Father and to the Son in eternal generation, the external works of the Trinity—which are inseparable—reflect this directionality. Once you see this directionality in the Gospel of John, there is no unseeing it. The Son comes *from* God the Father to do the works of God the Father. The Father never comes *from* the Son, because the Father is not eternally generated by the Son. The order of God's inner triune life is echoed in the order of God's triune deliverance.

Likewise, the directionality of the Spirit's work in the Scriptures is never reversed. Jesus tells us that the Father sends the Spirit in the Son's name (John 14:26), and he goes on to say that he himself will send the Spirit from the Father (John 15:26).

Furthermore, after his resurrection, Jesus *breathed* on the disciples and said, "Receive the Holy Spirit" (John 20:22). This is significant because the Spirit is described as *breath* or *wind* at an earlier point in the Gospel (John 3:6–8). If, then, the Spirit is divine breath, Jesus seems to be saying the Spirit is the *Son's* divine breath. The Son and Father are never said to be breathed out—or sent or poured out or given—by the Spirit, but rather the Spirit is breathed out by the Father and Son. Since the Spirit proceeds as eternally breathed out by the Father and Son, he is sent by the Father and Son in the work of salvation. Again, the order of God's inner triune life is echoed in the order of God's triune deliverance.

What we have seen here is but the surface of the scriptural revelation that teaches the Trinitarian dimensions of divine aseity—the mere froth and bubbles in the intoxicating draft of Trinitarian theology. But what our guide John has shown us is, I trust, enough for us to begin to revel in this fact: God has life in and of himself, and this life is an infinitely happy Triune life. The life of God is a boundless, ineffably wonderful fecundity—dynamic in his splendor and majesty—for it is ever from the Father, to the Son, and by the Spirit. Our God is infinitely happy! The Trinity is a bottomless ocean of vitality—spilling forth as the plentitude of life, light, and love. This, in short, is what it means for the triune God of the Scriptures to be eternal life.

7

Consume the Son and Live Forever

HAVE WE YET ARRIVED at a robust answer to my son's initial inquiry? Almost. We have established now—in humble and lowly terms—what it means for God to have life in himself. The eternal life of God is a fountain that flows from the headwaters of the Father and always and forever pours through the Son and in the Spirit. Never beginning and never ending, the triune God of the Scriptures is unceasingly blessed—happy in the simplicity of divine love that simply *is* Father, Son, and Spirit. The aseity of God means that God never diminishes in vitality even as he continues to give life to all so that there is a radical asymmetry between the life of God and the life God grants. God's life gives without emptying, enriches without impoverishing, and spills over without decreasing. Because this life everlastingly subsists in eternal generation (the Father begets the Son) and eternal spiration (the Father and Son breathe out the Spirit), God's dealings with his creatures take on this Trinitarian shape. Just as the life of God is eternally *from* the Father, *through* the Son, and *in* the Spirit, so too the salvation of God's people is *from* the Father, *through* the Son, and *in* the Spirit. Thus, the directionality of the triune mission portrayed in John's Gospel (the Son comes *from* the Father and goes back *to* the Father, bringing his saints with him *by* the Spirit) echos the directionality of the Trinity's inner life.

We ought not be surprised, then, to learn that the eternal life we come to experience comes *through* the Son, *by* the Spirit. "For God so loved the world," says the beloved disciple, "that he *gave* his only [begotten] Son, that whoever believes in him should not perish but have eternal life" (John 3:16). How is it that believing in the Son can become a means for having eternal life? Such is fitting because the Son is he who has been given to have life in himself (John 5:26). How is it that the Son can grant rivers of living water, which eternally satisfy our thirst for the life of God (see John 4:14, 7:37–39; Rev. 21:6)? Such is fitting because the Son is he who eternally breathes out the Spirit, whose presence causes the heart to "flow rivers of living water" (John 7:38).

Consider one more example from John's Gospel. John tells us of the feeding of the five thousand (John 6:1–15)—yet another occasion for the one who has life in himself to grant life to others. This physical feeding, however, was merely an object lesson for an infinitely better meal he was preparing for his people. The next day, when the crowd that had consumed his multiplied bread and fish found him, they came again seeking more culinary-related miracles. Jesus, knowing their intention (John 6:26), warned them of their shortsightedness: "Do not work for the food that perishes, but for the food that endures to eternal life, which the Son will give to you. For on him God the Father has set his seal" (John 6:27). Naturally, they ask what kind of work God has given them to do in order to receive such a marvelous food (John 6:28), and Jesus's answer is a paradox: "This is the work of God, that you believe in him whom he has sent" (John 6:29). The "work" is actually no work at all; it is merely to believe in the one whom the Father has sent—that is, the one whom the Father has eternally given to have life in himself.

The crowd can see, at this point, that Jesus is referring to himself, and so (with food still very much on their minds) they suggest that before they believe in him, he should prove himself in some way akin to Yahweh's provision of manna in the wilderness (John 6:30–31). Jesus responds with a revelation: As it turns out, the manna in the wilderness—just as the bread and the fish from the previous day—is also an object lesson. All this divine provision of bread is a sign from on high to call their attention from hungry bellies to hungry souls and their ultimate satiation found in the bread from heaven.

"Jesus said to them, '*I am* the bread of life; whoever comes to me shall not hunger, and whoever believes in me shall never thirst'" (John 6:35). In these few words, Jesus identifies himself as the breathtaking antecedent to two biblical referents: He identifies himself with Yahweh ("I am"), and he calls himself the true life-giving manna (cf. Ex. 16:15). In this way, we learn that God's purpose was always to bring not merely temporal sustenance with bread but to grant his people *eternal* life, and we learn that—wonder of wonders—he would grant this blessing with the provision of his very self. Again, the directionality in this whole scheme is undeniable. How will the *a se* Trinity grant eternal life to his people in the form of self-giving? Answer: in a way that accords with the Trinity's inner life. It will come *from* the Father and *through* the Son: "For this is the will of my Father, that everyone who looks on the Son and believes in him should have eternal life, and I will raise him up on the last day" (John 6:40).

Now, the crowds, noticing how central Jesus is making himself out to be for God's purposes to deliver his people, begin to feel a bit scandalized (John 6:41–42). Jesus, for his part, makes no attempt to dull the edge of his radical Christ-centeredness. He insists that everyone the Father intends to draw to himself he will draw, without exception, *to* Jesus and *through* belief in Jesus (John 6:43–49). With a crescendo, Jesus concludes his point by repeating his insistence that the manna in the wilderness had always been a foreshadowing of his own life-giving presence, except he now capitalizes on the surprising and almost grotesque language of eating flesh:

> Truly, truly, I say to you, unless you eat the flesh of the Son of Man and drink his blood, you have no life in you. Whoever feeds on my flesh and drinks my blood has eternal life, and I will raise him up on the last day. For my flesh is true food, and my blood is true drink. Whoever feeds on my flesh and drinks my blood abides in me, and I in him. *As the living Father sent me,* and I live because of the Father, so whoever feeds on me, he will live forever because of me. (John 6:53–57)

Can you sense it? Can you feel the mystery and holiness of Jesus's words and provision? Here we come to the burning heart of God's love for his people—an expression of God's self and the incorporation of his people *into* that love. God, who lives, gives himself to be consumed so that his people might live. How does he do this? The Father sends the Son in the flesh to give his flesh to be consumed by faith.

Of course, this passage reminds us of communion, and that is more than appropriate. Our Christian meal at the Lord's Table is, after all, a participation in the body and blood of Jesus (1 Cor. 10:16–17). In faith, at his table we partake of his body and blood, which are "true food" and "true drink" (John 6:55), and our communion with him is nothing if not life-giving. But at the core of this passage, Jesus refers to the eating and abiding reality of faith. To "believe" is, according to Jesus, to do the work of God and to eat the flesh and drink the blood of Christ. To consume and receive by faith his life-giving ministry is to eat the bread of life so as to live forever!

We know that the ultimate manifestation of the self-giving that Christ describes will come in his death on the cross. In dying, he makes himself the ultimate life-giving seed, which—after its burial—will sprout anew to produce all manner of fruit (John 12:20–26). We who would receive from his vitality must, therefore, learn to abide in him (John 15:1–17). The Son who has life in himself comes to us—he brings the life of God in the form of a man. He is a vine within our reach; he is bread we can consume; he is water that can quench our thirst.

Now, he has already told us that none of these things can possibly be ours unless we are born from above by the Spirit (John 3:1–15), which introduces a potential dilemma. How is it that we come to share in this eternal life? Do we receive it by the Spirit who brings us to Christ, or from Christ who gives us the Spirit? Well, it depends on where we are standing. From the standpoint of the divine economy, the Spirit—who wells up into springs of eternal life—is *given* by the Son. But from the vantage point of our experience of this life, the Spirit—who unites us to the life-giving vine—*brings* us to Christ. In the end, there is no contradiction: The life of God comes *from* the Father *through* the Son and *in* the Spirit, and so we come to share in this life *by* the Spirit *through* this Son and *before* the Father. God the Trinity comes to man to bring man to God the Trinity.

But we haven't thoroughly answered my son's good question yet: If God is eternal, which means he has no beginning and no end, and he grants eternal life to us who had a beginning, does that mean he is more eternal? Furthermore: If so, what does it even mean to say that our life is eternal if it doesn't mean the same thing as God's eternal life? In answering these questions, we must remind ourselves that all our talk of God—and, indeed, our being in relation to God's being—is analogical. Yes, God is *more* eternal. He is more eternal than the eternal life we are given in the same way that God is more than any other word we can apply to both God and ourselves. People can be "good," and God is "good." But his goodness transcends in every way the goodness of his creatures.

Our share in this divine life is always that of a creature participating in the likeness of God's aseity. God comes to man to bring man to enjoy the happy life of God. But in doing so, God does not obliterate man or absorb man into himself. In other words, our share in the life that God gives is always a life that is given and not our experience of coming to have life in ourselves. We never traverse from the creature side to the Creator side of the Creator-creature divide. Our delight in sharing in the life of God is always through Christ, in whom heaven and earth unite. As we are made in the image of God, our eternal life is in the image of God's aseity. This may seem like something of a letdown, but our persistent finitude means that our experience of eternal life is one of perpetual expansion. The only way for creatures to come to experience participation in the likeness of the divine is for their experience and delight of that infinite life to be everlastingly enlarged, forever and ever. Let us learn, therefore, to stand in wonder at the God who is. And let us come to delight in the fact that he is, indeed, infinitely more eternal than we ever will be. His eternality is the foundation for the eternal life we experience in Christ. Because we are finite and he is infinite, we can rejoice in the fact that our experience of eternal life will be marked by an increasing delight throughout this life and into the next, forever and ever.

> Glory be to the Father, and to the Son, and to the Holy
> Ghost;
> As it was in the beginning, is now, and ever shall be,
> world without end. Amen.

General Index

Scripture Index